The Fool
& The Bee

Also by Martin Corless-Smith

Poetry
Bitter Green (Fence Books 2015)
English Fragments: A Brief History of the Soul (Fence Books 2010)
Swallows (Fence Books 2006)
Nota (Fence Books 2003)
Complete Travels (West House Books 2000)
Of Piscator (University of Georgia Press 1998)

Fiction
This Fatal Looking Glass (SplitLevel Texts 2015)

Translations
Odious Horizons: Some Versions of Horace (Miami University Press 2019)

Martin Corless-Smith

The Fool & The Bee

Shearsman Books

First published in the United Kingdom in 2019 by
Shearsman Books
50 Westons Hill Drive
Emersons Green
BRISTOL
BS16 7DF

Shearsman Books Ltd Registered Office
30–31 St. James Place, Mangotsfield, Bristol BS16 9JB
(this address not for correspondence)

www.shearsman.com

ISBN 978-1-84861-644-8

ACKNOWLEDGEMENTS
The first act of *The Fool & The Bee* was published as a chapbook
by The Song Cave (NYC, 2018).
Withers was first published in *Equilibrium* (Boise, 2007)
Monadic Vistas was published in Colorado Review (Fort Collins, 2018)
and featured on *Poetry Daily*.

The prologue to *The Fool* appeared in an anthology made for
The Modern Hotel, Boise. Other poems have also appeared in
Cloud Rodeo and *Tarpaulin Sky*.

Thanks to those who read various versions of this book in manuscript:
Dan Beachy-Quick, Chris Violet Eaton, Alan Halsey, Fanny Howe,
Sara Nicholson, Boyd Nielson, Sasha Steensen, Cathy Wagner
and Kerri Webster.

Contents

I. The Fool & The Bee   9

II. Here Then at Last   73

III. Withers   85

IV. Monadic Vistas   91

The Fool & The Bee

I. The Fool & The Bee

A visionary processional in three acts

All myths born of a simple-shell,
All heroes born of a bee.

[Prologue]

That which was an Albatross
came sweetly down –
Alabaster artichokes on either side
the rendering of sky and sea
sufficient to supply the thought of Nature
in a fulgent mood – and Man at odds;
so audience and players might unite
suggesting human union transcends the solitude
of birds suspended (almost) endlessly above the void
– though how an hour or two of scenery
can hope to mimic an eternity…

…perhaps it is the ecstasy of Art
held temporarily between dark curtains
that proposes consciousness
played out on a human scale –
instrument of self and self's catastrophe.

Act I. Then

[Stage descriptive of an idyll]

[A scene opens]

Hark how it begins – a dollop of affection
played into atmosphere – a herring pointed at the Sun
All glittery – as if a talisman.
The herring now a symbol of out-fished oceans or

The herring now a name ill-known.
What shall I hold up to the Sun that might reflect
ironic glory – it is vain to think of cures
to superhuman tragedy – vain to think as well of carpet bombs and fasts.

I who have brought into my den the smirking fox
Disabused of charm and status in an urban realm
Now too like the poorer humans to elicit aught but fear
A loathing – entering the house obedient to need.

Where in the hierarchicals shall we place poetry?
A residue of culture when a story held us rapt –
or when a culture wrapped a farthing of anxiety
with prudent hope and anticipated ordin'ry resolve.

The sickness unto Death, The evils of Revolution
In consolation to his wife – Decline and Fall
Lord how shall we gather at the river
Without texting all our friends

Once in the enemy of time I rinsed my hate
with sadness made of Love and for a moment
found I could manage to exist without the burden
of anticipation answered by desire –

I could uphold the instances of being
as if by aspect they resolved all matter
into incidents that coincide – hold a herring to the Sun
Its eye a perfect mirror to the glory of the frozen present in a
            future memory.

*

…A pine grew through the centre of the house
and reached into the room – we could not
move so climbed up through its barbs
Out to a memory of stars…

…broken limbs that rests
Like a pier into the lake
a half moon with
Europe in the shadow of its other continents…

It was my body I saw climbing through
My house, my mother and my mind
The pine had been a thought hence out of time
It was as real as happiness

(The night that grew
with intermittent joy – a story with all hiding
lost at hand – rain and an ocean's wind
An eye inside the skull

which boats across the skein
Black depths – oil continent
Beauty of death her open look
And knowledgeless season

what energy drives one to move
On a limitless sea – towards what

Directionless motherless dream –
Skiathos or Helena – the trill

Of a single voice above the lapping
To tune immediate silence
Pizzicato archipelagos
Unseen – and what I crawled out to

Where I had ocean and secure
Where I had blood and celestial support
Out to a chainless step
And peer into the black liquor

Hopeless – travel where
We meet loneliness and
Anxious spills over to make
Me feel for her her outward

Incomprehensibility – an amazon of fear
Draws past a pine tree pyre
Born out of the glossy forest floor
Into its own oncoming gale

Field of seed drawn sideways draped
The wool of shepherd winters
A world to move across – transinfinite
The birth of something lost

Love like a great arched chasm
We find ourselves inside – remind me
Mother before you were – remind me
In our ocean above the roof

Where the splintered pine grows into night
Cold to the starry snows – pine
In an ecstasy of growth
A punt over a moat

For I don't know what I need to know
A pine on fire
The spirit of the house
A sacrifice for I don't know

A shadow candle burning down
Into the night for I don't know
My lover on another world
My mother and her mother too
A shudder through the empty room
I don't know I don't know).

Suppose this very now
An uproar is at hand
A visionary cleft
Through which to glimpse

Another ecstasy
The courts bemused
Seven restless youths
Have slit a bullock's throat

And was it sacrifice yet unordained?
Whilst you entomb yourselves
With ancient rites
No longer portents from the skies.

Called into being as if invited to some festival
Some custom of restraint, some instinct of excess
The pears near bruised with succulence
The liquor pouring thickly down the legs

Oh there is no tomorrow after sacrifice
It is another world held open for the revelers
The great-winged beetle is above us now
Held there by breath and dream alone.

What of the idiot king – shocked at his dismissal?
What of the well-schooled Dame?
Feed the horses – empty the barrows
No one shall be subject to their dues.

What pleasure bibes the clown?
Columbine's dream
Being a fly mid-stream
No fate, no fears, no views.

We have thought up a story so intricate
There cannot be a plot.
We have peopled the cities with characters
Who all believe their act.

Not the Martial arts, nor the bee alone
Not the horse and chariot, nor the monstrous snake
Here is the indifferent squid – here the rising mold
Here the sensuous toadstool hidden in its gloom.

[Enter the hermaphroditic spirit sublime, a poet crowned in myrtle]

for Alan Halsey

I misread arms for anus – errors for eros
Misheard the red moon flakes
Which means precisely nothing
Pre-cise-ly.

Angel abuts the church ceiling
At such and such an angle, faith!
Where calmness and calamity
Mix heresy with hearsay.

The wary flower
Kissed so sweetly
By wind and bee
Kiss again so wearily

[Enter Mars-Ares]

The hacking cough, throat
Eye down the face like egg
Blood not staunched
These boys into the face of that

I can't help hide but
Where shall we swallow
Hate or fear – the boy
Whose beaten face resembles

Love – poured into nowhere
perfunctory responses are professional
I can't help but hide
My own fear and privilege

That's my son, some man
is everybody's son, why can
we let it go – not ours
how can it not be though.

[Enter Bee-Aphrodite, the twins embrace]

Breast of an Amazon
The boyhood figure
Lean, confused against
The empty chair.

What when your parents
Leave the empty house
What when the tepid bath
You sit into

She will have grown a cock
Sister to your own
Curved like a gourd
To slip into yr groan

Only her face will show
Her shock at having grown
This erection ripe
Unearthed from lust – a thirst burst

Out at last – a deity born of the root
The roof caves in
The mouth caves in
The shout to no-one new….

Bare feet across the kitchen floor
Sweet lichor down the thigh
On marble tiles
Now puddles underfoot.

Incestuous self
Hung on a limb
The penetrant's penetration
Death coiled around her maiden.

Sick in the heat
Victorian
Mahogany
Horse hair settee

Collapsible cellophane pink
Her pale flesh green
The cork released
From the medicine flask

This cold pink silk
Is wet – this cold slate grey
Sky seen through the door
Of the scullery

Incestuous salt
The tender lamb
Lean on her knee
The sleeping swoon

Winter in spring
The cradle blooms
By fireside
The flood emerge with charred footprints

At your age, your age
At your age emerge
Into the cold
Of a strange kitchen.

Slick potato peel
Heel of foot
Pierced by
A rusty screw.

*

towel robe, jowled mutt
drools by OT prophet
Jowett of Balliol under a puppet
Grass stained knees bent for eternity.

[the two halves of the goddess wander the city]

sweet virgina sweet faustina
lips bit her legs the other parts
how can a sister helper
fail down on her knees apart

crowd in Broad Street
crave an alley
crack in the open
hand on your pulley

whisper it open
finger her smile
taste of vinegar
wish it wide a while.

[Enter marching guards]

Stamping veldtschoen
Stumbles o'ver – war march
The empty gesture borders
Ignorant obliterating laugh.

[marching continues off stage]

*[Enter a diminutive genderless figure
with wild red hair, dressed accordingly]*

for Algernon Swinburne

Pushing his cart down Gray's Inn Road
Tittuping along High Holborn
A ghost in the traffic of Tottenham Court
His head in a lofty realm.

A "cupido crucifixus on a chair of anguish"
Collapsing (silk hat) in the Art Club lavvy
Hunted by Nanny Age 34
From flagellation brothels to the British library

Poet ahoy – face first out the Hansom
Majestic in spite of his fall
The stage of poetry too high to replace
With aught but his lemon and brandy drill.

*[figure fades into shadow, a smoking figure in
flamboyant scarf emerges]*

for Stephen Rodefer (from a line by Jean Calais)

And taking one last gulp of dark red wine
He outward span into eternity
(or if too grand) he fell
the paving opened in a yawn
and heaven shat its arms
                    around his neck
anyone who loves, anyone who
gives up anything for love
is liable to disasters of this kind.

[...replaced by bulky ageing biker in spurs]

after Jonson

Drop drop the daffodil
That until now
Had loved itself full well
Your face has lost
Its golden boast
An echo of its glow

Drop drop dear Narcissus
Who once was loved true well
The noon has passed full overhead
And you must pass as well

Droop droop wet buttercup
That never bloomed so well
That down
The rain that fell upon
The minute sun
Will shrivel
Its face up

[*…now a dandy Mod*]

[*each ghost-poet a poem*]

How long shall this like dying life endure —Spenser

How long shall dying live like this
A short chair we shall crouch upon
An edge no rest an ache a duration
Better were it fit to go but with no direction
Wait endure uncertain of our destination
We in this crowded room just sit.

(Like an Historian with relics broke
we assemble who we are from bits
that crumble in our grasp and
had no story til we spoke of them).

after Lucian

Death in his boat
With sail and oar
Listen to my song upon the beach
Death who the poet
Sang to in his grief
With words to sooth the tiger and the boar.

Death with his tusk
Death with his tooth & claw.

Carry me over to the other shore

So sang the poet in his grief
A song to match the nightingale's lament
Hence went his lover with one bite
from hidden adder on her fleeing foot
Bring me to her that travelled far
over the deep and troubled main.

Seven pelican take flight across the sand
Silent beneath the sun
Over the ocean roar
Frigate birds encircle the invisible and

Death in his boat with sail and oar.

[the sound of snow falling on the sea]

Lady of Shalott

How was your evening turning
Anger into love or sadness
Once arriving out of doors
To tour a room – we meet others

And declare – decide – demur
I cannot find a goat out in the lake
I'll try to hold this candle still
It's madness to concoct a life
With you or without you.

Did you see the mouth emerge
Like an open eye – to say
s/he as my other – allow me
a bottom in the gallery.

L'inconnue de la Seine
She's not enticing
She's dead, the skin drawn
Into an imperfect smile

It takes a little
Imagination
To desire the dead
your needs require

[final poet-shade meanders dockside]

Seeing but nothing outside self
The parallel lives lived silently
Through unsensed universal veins
An ocean floating through the sea

Black dark blank – tissued vessel
Floated flooded south
Here at the fo'c'sle wall
Word left the ear before the mouth

Dearth in plenitude – farcical vanity
Production overwhelming all – the past
For once seemed longer than
the future.

[distant intermittent foghorn]

[Nemesis hovers above Threadneedle Street]

early mortality – fuck you
patron of the ark – arch – arse
patted on its way – up
thanksward to the cusp

voracious oleanders – rhododendrons – kelp
algae glooms – mud flies & hero salt
child falls at the beach
wealthy doners kneeling to one side

mortification of salt
delusion of rain and gales
tides besiege ranges & plain
forests go weak at the knees

[bells over the city]

[air raid siren]

A nighttime broadcast
From somewhere in the Netherlands
Announcing something in a foreign tongue
That nonetheless we understand

A rolling catafalque
Heaving its own corpse
Like a mouth swallowing
Its own mouth

The earth's double pneumonia
Sends coughs and gasps
To ostrich ears buried under
ossifying glass

The endless migrations ended
In desert swamps – mosquitoes
Fell the final beasts
The open skull a feast for all of us

Help opens fantasies of green
Lush gardens saved in green houses
Slumbering eternal vacuums
Filled with jars and drawers of ancient specimens

Cracked at the door
Poor soil
Fried lizard like a root
On dusty floor

Heartness dark wandering
Blown like cicada wing
Over the tender eye
Blue into blue eternally

A torn canopy crow wing
Cosmological synapse in
Glorious lapis with gilt inlay
Or ormolu errancy

Rising ash sails funereal
Jackdaws furious laughter or
Rarely cawing response – inches
Of strokes. The body lifts

Liquid crowds – liquid reply
In language's black feathers
Curved as in flight
Night written over clay.

Beech trees seconded
Avenue of limes
Rare willow conspicuous in
Such handwriting.

[Poetic interlude]

On yellow foolscap or onion skin
(the Olivetti or the Pelikan)
record the dark hair
of a future lover
You I love
You say to me
as if one day
were possible
compost for flowers –
what's rather grand,
once in the ground:
All powers gone – All darkness indivisible.

The panic of the young companions

Sotto voce

Just hold that
I beg you
I won't
I'm so close

Just once
For you only
I can't
It's too much

[Exit Spirit of Poetry, glimpse of attendant fool off stage]

two eyes
upon the beach
the fool's face
disintegrates

years of tears
salt waves
he thinks
makes oceans seas

the glitter
that he sees
are stars

he sees the moon
a paper arc
he sits upon

he hears the wind
his breath
he sings between

the mordant duck
the curious ape
this morbid rock
dropped in a lunascape!

[Poetic interlude]

[young child riding the back of an ancient turtle]

History

there is of course
little of nothing
to tell. The boy on the bank
or the bridge – dressed
in different clothes
indifferently –
the small theatre of the water surface
reflection – dimpled – collaging
sky blue with dark green foliage
then, somehow, beneath the cold
three feet down below
the golden shale
bed of the stream
so that one sees on one surface
the sky, the trees, the stream itself
and the bottom of the brook –
all in exchange – moving and staging
charging back and forth –
water over earth

add then to this
the instant of a passing bird
as if the spectacle was
beyond reckoning and so
was so precise and quiet
that one could only half
experience it – the memory was not
of a conscious event. Nothing
of intent or reckoning –
the flash of blue split the
reverie of stream.

Act II. Here

[Stage descriptive of recently abandoned camp]

[Enter a chorus of festival singers]

And the narwhal hangs from the Christmas tree
And the blue glass fish and the Chinese bird
And the wooden house with no one in
And I who hang them there beneath

And I'm lay down in a nest of needles
Pine sweat gluing wool and hair
And only wind to call me after
Rain and soon another year

*

IN the spring there is great rejoicing
great sorrow and great rejoicing
floods carry off the settlements – and in the thaw
absconded uncles hanging under eaves.

(the shrill neighs of deserters as
hunting dogs upon them in the woods)

*

the devil swore twice he'd take you
the devil swore twice he'd not
the devil rode past on a blind black horse
and rushed to his nether plot

he stole the dress from a washing line
he stole the heart of a bride
who dreamt of a life away from home
with a life at another time

*[Enter the figure of Edward Thomas dressed as Achilles, holding a
fob-watch in front of his heart...]*

The forest is
icumen in
the dreadful swallows
fill the sky
so happily so dreadfully
so dread so dread
so merrily

when just a bird
against the wall
but 7,000
in the arc
across the air
from field to fair
so dark so dark
so merrily

the soldier is
a sprightly bird
that drones
in sequence over hills
that used to sing
so wearily
so lost lost
so merrily

an iron countenance
she had
to show the world
her enmity
the ghost unsettled
in her bed
so dread so dread
most merrily

*

(A hundred years
since WWI
an hundred years
and its not done
or gone – or won
nor fucking won
nor wonderful nor wonderful
nor ever even meaningful

my rose garden
is never mine
though I might one
day see its face
it is too late
to place a rose
or own a place

Left with the wird
outside the counsel door
or left with the outside
wandering – the right to
non-conform – impossible
we break open atrocities
here in our own cities)

*

The dust and shadow
left behind
the body heat
upon the screen
the lead balloon
dismantled mine
someone expels
so merrily

[…his body is lifted by an exploding shell]

*[Slowly disintegrating corpse, vines erupting
through what was once the mouth]*

The greenman

A bee upon the beard
When the steeple fell to earth
The village shrank in fear
Such omens rare

A bee upon the beard
Where shall a hive
The skull out in the field
A bullock's grave

A bee upon the beard
The angel seen
At night out in an elm
Calling the prophet's name

A bee upon the beard
Shall be the only sign
And when the day has come
We'll gather there to leave

A bee upon the beard
Of mistletoe beneath
The jackdaw's ratty nest
A gold and silver wreath

The elderflower bloom
Of white and fragrant lace
a collar for
the greenman's feral mask

the wind through oak and ash
and rising from the ley
of scrappy crows and trash
all over the wash

and all over the wash
the flooding fords and stream
no island in the flash
no bee upon the beard

from satan-in-the-wold
to robin-in-the-wall
the waters rise as one

are held above the ground
the seagulls at arm's length
on daylight's green ague
held out into harms way

the sacrificial knees
torn open
graze beneath
on dismal weeds

his barked face wretching green
the tongue screams into leaf
a beautiful tree-littered heath
where murder has been felt

mole rag vole rot
dam reft
arc ox fuck wagon box
treft grazz fue, graz fraie

[Exuent players to the right; to the left a temporary
frieze of Europa reclining on an English shore]

Ilfracombe (her last holiday)

Concerning smoke
& sundry shades
psalms for indifferent ears
charms for indifferent days

mistress in the prime of lust
a cloud of doubt
a clot of blood
opens her night coat

black ships before Ilfracombe
black spiders crawl up Linton Hill
(funicular down to Lynmouth)
midmorning curtains drawn

Dame Cynthia will lend her light
Time to lie across
pale-faced with feral death
only what is past is real.

Fado accordion's
forlorn tune (a spider plant
in green aquarium)
Boxwood acorn on the mantlepiece

Black sails before Ilfracombe
Black slick Lisboa street
Sea like an oyster shell
Dark with white spits

[sound of gulls]

[Followed by various scene shifts, perhaps memories of the poet-fool]

Hadzor (Dutch Brethren)

It were as if the scarecrow
Ought function as a windmill
The cross cut down, the oats ground
The old coat worn next season.

The grass ticked tickled
Under the towering elm
Under the limes and elms
And the day rolled lazily on

I felt no sound, heard no fly
For seconds of for months
And winding there under the bough
I died quietly and so.

*

Balthus in Rome

To the unknown God of unachieved desire – Swinburne

Golden aroma of
Beautiful plain girl
Naked in youth
Small golden tuft
Nobody should see
Thee sea snails and
Piccolo pink shells
Picked from the sofa
Tray & mirror
Afternoon my cat
Yawns in velvet
Whether I wear a gown
Or not – the little

Finch in a box
Flutters to remind
Us of our death
Couped in a cage
For nary a year
Why help us to hold
Up a thin gauze
Drawn across a
Rump – the warm
Viscosity a toe
In mud
A finger in the mouth
Eyelids hardly raised
To her fey funeral.

*

Salwarpe

Because I am not
Around other people I forget
My childhood and my dream
Of happiness away from other people.

Did I mean to survive
Childhood this long
So that now I must live
anew or revive some memory

Roast chicken on Sunday
After a walk – the lychgate
Warm in the sun – we
Make it home late.

*

Margate

I take that cloud to be
Myself in the form of a rabbit
Dissolving as soon as beginning
A tea biscuit dunked in the tea.

Christ might have said
A lot of things before
Transforming into wine
And bread and then vanishing

The symbol of myself
Was thrown into the sea
As if to regenerate
Me on my trip to Margate

A protagonist waded in the bladderack
And scum towards an ideal
While his lover flounders
Back to safer ground and flees

Judging my distance by a wreck
(the king's drowned father), out
further than I expected
the buoys all livid, bouncingly reflected.

*

Barcelona (Monarch wings reconstructed)

Venus, mercurios, torsos de atletes
Cariatides y apolos in midnight magenta
Herein the vaults of absent gods – blue
Electric silver dust – the sea rolling its gold

In the murky brine – a windowless machine
Goats mirthless with laughter the old orchardos
Ynglish e skeleton grins in grimeworld a youth
Holding a thumb and index indicates the lost pebble
Revolving in an obscene universe of cinder green (a vert)
Regalo replica without anecdotes narcotic parasols/perabolas
Boys that live in authenticated liveries & porticos.

Plant by the table – Jhe planets of Joy & Sadness
Greys & White & Yellow plaid cedar cavern & chest
Cough of the youthful parrot Christ with the twelve other
Christs with a shovel and an elbow in the heat
Yoruba y Jalisco y Nakiwa Abominable venues
Such as these. Japonica Tea whiskered shadow
Sparrow Hill and Swallow dale – The Vale of Hallowed
Paper docents. Frail marble faunus y falcones
Hospital bed where consciousness accesses frescoes
Of lone wolf on plaster field and ceiling rose
Marmoles del Partenon a Londres.

[raucous green parrots]

Kew Gardens

The Thames-daughters, arm in arm
Along the embankment – the city barge
For lunch, then Kew more drink
Ridiculous in Piccadilly pink, size XL.

It is my last day, it is always my last day
Again – how long can this go on.
My son and I exhausted on the plane
But somehow 1930's England will remain.

A boat floats into view
We must save the world from suicide
Another boat, a jetty
We decide to abandon dinner plans

Only the wind's at home
In Kensington (& Chelsea)
Developers lope in pairs and
Foreign parakeets screech

A poem of drouth and despair
Incongruous in today's demotic speech
Where chatter like the birdies
Speaks apocalypse and war.

Lips and hair, shorts barely
Passing down Old Brompton Road
I'm old – I'm hardly there
Or here, spread over decades

The decadence of self-reflexion
My last indulgence – whence
Off to meet my older generation
One or two surviving the decay.

And so another summer swallows
Up again completed, spreads into
The past, concertina'd in the shape
Of one long summer day.

*

Kinsham

At dawn to see the cabbages
The sky rising in every drop
On purple leaves on golden purple
Frost on frozen window panes

Wet shoes wet trouser cuffs
Will dry along hot Oxford Street
For I will leave today
And never see these cabbages again

*

The West End

The fires of Piccadilly
Circus master gutters
tainted flags and conflagrations
hungering the alleyways

take an aspect of the scene:
a dog reads tarots
for a Queen – it's painted
in the manner of Corot

for avant-gardist parlours.
In the street street cleaners clean
The coffeeshop debris
in after-riot of post-carnival sobriety…

…so Hurricanos executing fires singe my white beard
thick round world floats in canal
basin falls as rich folk empty
Harrods foodhall foods

*

The City under Construction (the Diggers)

Giovanni's verduto
engraves the tower of Bishopsgate Without
A greenfinch sweets across St. Georges Hill
to level common ground

Laughter is heard down St. Giles
Morning appears in the skies
Come home cries as evening falls
Along the underpass

[One ancient figure dressed as a child steps forward]

This wrinkled globe's soft rolling in wan light
with sere angels crackling beneath
the ocean spread out over an abyss
a raft of silver foil above a coral reef

[Poetic interlude]

[Venus appears dressed as Demeter wearing a rent-veil and crown of Damascene water-lilies with cucumbers from the Nile]

Dear small world (an orange): A letter from the country

Exiled whether by or not by
choice — here's where voice
finds starts and stops — gasping
fruit — dear small exhaustible
somewhat known by name,
new life warmed bound up in ice
such as will welcome
soft numbers of the self
Lovers shut up in a sign
happiness delivered through
grateful & hasty recognition
undress our meaning
like an orange from the ground
       The sweetness should
hold nourishment that such
fragrance proves — resembling
a kind of fate — the glorious
disrobing — blossom falling
into juice — garlands for our grave
Why else live in such artificial arbors
ink scorning beauty as a ruse
our negligence must wear a gown
and serious leisure be careless
showing little thought — trees
planted prior to our needs
wasted days the objection
to necessity and oblivion
as if our trivia
were proof to waste the ruin
of presiding death — a laugh

to disengage disease – hang
thus a mirror on
distempered walls – for all
we have outside of Nature's gifts
is the chance to give such gifts away.

Act III. At last

[Scene of an empty theatre. Evidence of an after party]

[Enter the fool singing a dirge to his own accompaniment]

A bee song

Dead bee Astronaut
who disappears in to the night
how can your dust
be brushed aside

You dance under a sun
just like the myths
where gods fought out stories
to explain our drought

The last light flickers
of the town as
we spread on to moors
the darkness like a carcass

Out of the lion's skull
the green tin said
we'd porridge for some sweet
December night

Only a beeping now
can raise the dead
from radio silence
once we tune them out

I'm waiting for the last
bus home – although

the road has sunk
into a cake

We'll throw out time
and dust into the atmosphere
our song – and not
be here to hear it rhyme.

[the fool who is the jester, the jack, Hermes, Mercury…]

The Fool's dream

In a crystalled dream impossible
to recall how the past unearthed a craft
named Mercury – poisonous quick silver wit
aimed at the moon's alternative

native to earth yet separate
the fool digests all emptiness
until uplifted to a realm that
questions answering

It took a century to realize
Earth had died inside
a tin cup left upon a wall
the slowworm struggled in the glare until the hawk arrived.

[…an hallucination so various it might encompass the universe]

[Proscenium decorated with a canopy of shells and alluvial detritus, absent goddess implied.]

The Birth of Venus (The Poet's Lament)

With the face of a fish you come into the light
Silvery scaled as it seemed
Shaded by a cardboard crown
With the face of a lemur wide-eyed

All pomp and purpose due
To this exalted scallop dish
A line of willow-maids
A chorus of boys draped in blue

Here in my mauve padded tunic
against the canopy top
semi-gems in myrtle settings
A horse in its panoply clad

She assumes the shape of a seal
She wanders the crimson land
In a scarf wrested from a guard
With a trident and fish garland

Serving the new-born Venus
rooks crow to announce the dawn
Serving the liver of the grey-fleshed poet
Grey-suited, grey-haired, forlorn.

The centaur rises in the stone
Stolen from a former world.
Eclipsed by fashionable LPs
backdrop to the nymphs' iPhones.

Negronis irrigate the night
blast bugles beneath the floor
A headlight wipes the stucco wall
Then falls off down the street

The osteria basement reeks of wool
church mold, mildew, decayed wood.
The river hasn't risen in decades now
Praise the linguine with clams.

The Ardent Fool

The spirit of a bird recalled
along the dun canal
A kingfisher in velvet slacks
withdraws immediately

On the edge of Arden
born in a swoon
On the fringe of Feckenham
Under a bomber's moon

floodlit for the Luftwaffe
A stage for rural games:

The fabled forest Poetry
amidst the real and generated fog
a dressing room for clowns dressed for
the re-enactment of a war

transformations are not found
in cities or in palaces.
Such coffer-realms are made of stone
a morgue-fugue for the phalanxes

burning their own houses down
to bake a mealy loaf
or hold a foreign clown in chains
to torture at the gates.

The water in the lane enflames
the gas works & the pub
pollarded men in undershirts
dig coal and rice and snow

We'll go to bed in green & red
upon the forest floor
where blanket snow and sooty ash
will sooth us in its glow.

[Distant sound of dogs barking]

I can't help seeing what has happened
as a waste of everything – entropy & thanatos
& pathos & regurgitated paint,
Everyone I meet's as worthless as I am.

I'd daub more if my sight were good
Hear more if I could – instead
I'm left to tend the embers of an average fire
Unprepared to blow it into life again.

The coughing of car doors
climate change & orchestras.
The sweet black earth in our back yard
no good for anything but cress

At times I could not see the blood
of Christ smoked from a clay pipe bowl,
a glass *dame-jeanne*, a green carboy
of sulphates and bone meal

We built a cart
from broken prams
and raced down hill
in thrilled alarm

And then one boy killed a pigeon
then shot a neighbour's son
His mother played the organ
His father sang:

Somedays by the bank
Waiting for
Somedays in the house
No idea

Perhaps I lost an eye
or an arm – and the day
didn't end the way we planned

Perhaps I fell down
laughing in the gutter
out of exhaustion & utter failure

Tablets on the table
mother dead now
seems inevitable though.

[The fool dressed as a drone]

A fool's dance

Enter the fool dressed as himself
A doublet doubting even that
Where on the stage is right to stop
The spirit's state is tottering

Make me an omelette of all that
The world, the weft, the woebegone
You cannot break an egg
Without making one

Your world is balanced on an ant
Or on a teabag on a shelf
A penny drops into the lake
And wakes crossover on themselves

Make nothing out of nothing and you cease to live
Make anything and still you cease
I have increased my daily output by a factor close to nil
It's not a lot but it does show my intent

Grasping at apples grasping at forks
I'll never have the end of it
A cup that dribbles as it walks
Away with all my drink in it.

[Venus dressed as Britannia on her royal barge,
holding aloft a single oar]

Anchored in the Thames since
The last year of the nineteenth century
Ready to depart
Into imagery, disease & poetry

A creature spilling over every bank
the slipways rinsed of evidence
the seagulls mostly still
upon the long sunk barge slung rank among the effluence

The desert under every tree
The city and the flooded tides
Abandoned underneath the skin.

[Venus dressed as Queen-Bee wearing a gas-mask]

The fool's dance is a fever
Those denying hope all gather here
To weep against themselves
A unicorn trapped in a tapestry

I stumble at the teetering brink
To clamber out of burning fields
Where polished floors & ashen tiles of the removed farm house
Are crumbled over stubble rows

The greenhouse glass
Has all been smashed
For no good reason
I can find

With nothing to repay the dawn
Just glittering reflection of debris
We wait until we feel more certain
Along the beach drive wall, behind the camper van curtain

The back of light falls off the sky
an angel crushed into the space between
a day unfurled – alive and alone
a girl you loved so much you called her every day

Let the hearer be named
Alone on the strand
With no one to tell
An ear to the shell

[The fool and the bee dressed as Venus and Mars]

A roman chanticleer
Have we not wings before we walk?
Before we run a path – before we wake
A day – blown into necessity from dust

Up rose the image of a memory
Black sacking in the soil
Shape of a crow, but when you pull
It is a tarp grown under growth.

The house's shroud
Oiled and frayed
Passing from one scene
To another we embrace
The florid sky and
Dapples of the sun-dazzled ash

Where the vole goes there go I
Betrothed to earth and greenery
The nettles and queen anne's lace
That must up stock and history

I shall die in a kitchen midden
pekoe leaves and orange peel
The recent dregs of recent meals
The sanctuary of the past unhidden

Golden spiders at the centre of their webs
Their abdomens like bulbs in early light
Here is a gift of anonymity
Sheltered in the stray wood of the shed

The jungle trout
The mountain thrush

Where nothing is suggested in the way of order
Thinking of Sligo and drinking water.

[Figure of an elderly man in a Chesterfield coat and Homburg]

[Poetic interlude]

[At 'The Dead Swan and Colander,'
pub sign painted in the style of Tiepolo]

<u>*In Error*</u>

Feckless middle-old
trounced by sorrow
Jolly's older brother
laid up on a couch
Illiterate in self and other
studies – gone
quite at the knees.
Deliver him from
Selfhood's own exaggerated realm –
Drowned in fermentation
indefatigably barking.

And the old man cannot afford a maid
With black rolling cloud of scintillas
Abandoned flotillas spreading
The dog lying prone on the grave.

[Poetic interlude]

[Fool holding the dead bee in his palm]

Much like the seely bird
I do not much care anymore
So now I sing – no note of joy
That hears the partridge beat her wings
Her dark disdain for my shrill tune
More like a ghost than anyone
My sadness will eclipse the sun
Casting shade against the ground
To show where we have gone.

Departing the City

Stranger if I had loved you
You were unfaithful
The sirocco blows over the south
Bound platform on the Northern Line

If we had fucked, you were
Somebody else's lover
I go to famous places but
The faces in the pub are real

Down Fleet Street in company
Up to Lincoln's Inn we
Separate at Drury Lane
And we are free again

A thin sheet between us
And an infinite night –
Atlantic, choppy for the top thirty feet
Atmosphere, then stars.

It's true I have destroyed the world
Just by living – by uttering truths
And falsehoods – leaning across to
You, solemn, killing worlds

The Sea of Japan
Bitter taste at the end
As if a fin rose in the waste
A black mouth gaping

[Poetic interlude]

[Projection of the fool and the dead bee dancing]

<u>*A labyrinthine description of a thing without content*</u>

Express desire in the colour that it first appears – European Alder
lines the scrappy path – where in company a flycatcher
or nightingale remains invisible//once when a visit
to the grand estate paid off. She loved me for one day//
Antwerp at 4 a.m. or other places he has never been
a continental breakfast hours before the coach takes off
the giftshop open for Academy of Art knick-knacks
day after Guy Fawkes day the carcasses of fireworks
litter playing fields – leavers picnic in their personally adapted uniforms
the past happens again and we are resolute
we will not miss a second this time round
the fault of being in a rush to notice and attend
as bunting snags the washing line – pearls
in a raffle for the school – pearls that are pale
and plastic blue (donated by a parent for a parent via a child), part of
a clown's kaleidoscope, the fax delivered is illegible
perhaps it is a drawing of a shed or else a letter of rejection
from a future you already packed up for. Please do not attend for
         interview.
Red brick ex-dairy renovation – walls suspended
over concrete floors – radiator paint in bronze and sash
grey windows. Mostly Art just looks like reclaimed junk
because it is.
There is a mud outline – a lurid green depicts his speech
of drunken self-promotion in a corduroy affair – it is the task
of every man to make rehearsal last as long as
every willing extra will participate – the back of the head
is royal blue – the cheeks and ears are pink –
then rises music from the floor – cantatas of bombast
huge Germanic Orchestra – and then release. Good.
Now try again.

When was the last time a relationship
maintained a critical amount of necessary satiety...
when was the ebb turned flow
and plastic bottles overtook the population on the beach?
Gull cried its mournful-crack absurdity
to anybody listening – eyes blistered by the sand
and stories made extraordinary histories seem ordinary.
The small degree of increase & decrease
is indiscernible as toddlers practice ice-cream eating
on the promenade. Suddenly you see the flow has ebbed.

Grand seeming small fruit tree
whose ugly winter scrabble
shimmers in the halo of green canopies
white floaty baubles
froth unhemmed for Ovid's sudden
transformation-tragedy. It turns out
well in the end. There isn't one.
The drawing room is aired
and ready for the seasonal retreat
of dying sons. The eyes are chlorine green
the dogs are on the green – the green is green
we seldom sleep these days
here where we always wanted to end up – here
where we started, stalled, exaggerated, left.
Here where one never can
relive the prior instant or relieve
the action of its consequence.
Man, being timely, sticks in time
no counterpart alternative survives
just memory, receding with each play
of counterfactual chances – ghosts
that never walked the house
                              haunt everyday.

A poet's dream

Outside the J.J. Gibbons shopfront
The tannoy pumping Opus 141
The paving slabs upright again reveal
God expressing love for everyone

Canoptic vases wander past
Aurochs standing in corrupted sties
The fervent spring of Queen May's temperament
Under the city's noxious aureate sky

"it is all too beautiful!" she cries
from the backseat of her passing car
crimes committed cannot alter this
the tragic and the poor are passing too

The Poet's Lament (The Birth of Venus)

Poor Auden – to be himself
much smaller in life than in fame
I looked at his almost shame
a humpf at surviving his book

Anglers punctuate the tidal edge
and dippers run the back and forth
where nacreous absent froth evaporates
receding and then pulling back to shore.

The ray twirls in uninhabited darkness
which is not so – many millions etc.
& floodlit arrival, I cannot ever be away
which wishing – but shit – I sit down here

it was a Friday or such and I thought
yes we might reach heaven etc.
but it was the next day after
and so a poem finishes

[Exuent fool and bee with flowers strewn]

[Poetic epilogue]

[Bee-Fool-Mars-Venus, her chariot dragged into the rising ocean, carries a placard announcing: "All myths born of a simple-shell / All heroes born of a bee."]

The Deluges

What happens is
difficult to say
one way or another
we piece together
what has, after all
already passed.
Take for instance
A life, or a part
of one played out.
A love affair/most commonly
considered necessary
a family – relationships
that constitute a self
school life – a series
of forgotten holidays
and dawn
four birds sing concurrently
cardinal and crow
chickadee and sparrow
truck reversing
sky revealing sun
catbird then wren
best when
London morning
M4 traffic,
Heathrow –
The village stirring
Who will love me
Who will pay me

Memorabilia
The streets grow
Mitochondria
Herringbone design
Tweed jacket
Lost a pocket
"last a lifetime"
such as this –
Romayne grew dawn
Out in her garden
Once again
The kitchen door wide open
For the air
The local strays
Grey clouds above
Great cherry trees
And limes
The robins and the squeaking pies
Occasional jackdaw
Or later when the day is old
The hirundines in gangs
Sweet whistles past the house
The open windows
For another London evening
The trucks reversing
Building endless need
Oh holy war
Where in the scheme of this
Shall we succeed.

II.

Here Then at Last

Here then at last. Again. His Magnus Opum – Oposthumous possum wreackage of a piece – if there has to be forgiveness – and if there has to be retributions, tribunals and if, after all is said and done (and not said nor done) ignored in a way that suggests either it is too late or it is not good enough, simply put: a life wasted at an ill-fitting task – a waste of time, of a life – a vast vanity pantomime played to an audience of nil – well, sobeit.

After all – what else, given the options he was given – what else raised its mitt – bothered even to lie there complacently to be noticed or overlooked? What did? Nothing, or nothing much. Born at a time when things had seemed possible – possibly even a time of national even international confidence – now, fifty, fucking fifty, five zero years later no. Now – nothing seems about right.

A calamity and a calumny. A catastrophe of microlithic proportions. A doodle in the stream. Begin.

Once when a boat was pushed without much ado into the late evening current – a darkling meadow of main stretching its yawn over to the distant shale – heron, still stalking crepuscular – and a moon already bobby in the flat plane sky. Awful how infrequently one now even attempts a new experience. Imagining a life of repeats or perhaps living one. Here – at dusk – a boat – without remark, out into the what-must-be-freezing tow towards the coastal estuary. Here I might like to die.

Fat dowager on skinny belligerent moped. Owl from the spinney to the vet's – imp wing feather followed by chocolate popcorn from Pershore Thorntons. A vision of sudden death – as she drives past the post office van – herself above herself – as she drives past the post office van – fata morgana – fatal in the air mirroring herself – "this" she asks "is it?" This is it, an instant doubled – and thus its own other – here self is self's other – and consciousness exhausts itself infinitely in the instant. Here is my life and death – well then, let's see how long the möbius strip attributed to this final moment lasts.

The English mail coach – Maidenhead to Gravesend.

This weekend, set in motion before weekends existed, before Brutus founded England and the Druids flew their drones over the Henge. The Throckmortons had always lived here – literally and metaphorically. Ideas, unlike commonly thought – arrive not through the trials of logic, but through a transfusion of the kernel via the trivial apparatus of thinking. Nothing that ever is, wasn't.

An important pair of George III giltwood girandoles – made for Mr. Throckmorton in 1764 – Always here in the hall – always reflecting upon each other the importance of such permanence. Agrippa's vision! Here we see Rachel weeping, here Medusa stony-faced from the premises in Cheapside – no longer fitting.

Where in shadow of the hallway is the door? Opens to a lawn which is never used, other than to be looked upon. Its importance is that it is never used. We have land aplenty – even if the ha-ha admits otherwise.

Minerva over life-sized, marble. Which way round is the chicken? One of course surviving quite famously without its head for a number of years. The keys are in the Qing. A sleeping hermaphrodite or a rampant centaur – both speak of stasis and disruption. Portals of trans-formation.

Torching the gutted mansion will save time and (thus?) money. Had my equanimity been challenged, poisoned by some trivial encounter?

Yes, perhaps, but no. The fool, as we know, lives alone. The patter of his footsteps along the carriageway, the cobbles, the courtyard are echoes of earlier fancies, dances, galliardes. Later still the Mazurka, the cakewalk – the trot!

Sarabandes & chaconnes – here upon his toes in socks the earth is marked in magical escape, the temple of Minerva, the labyrinth at Chartres – the Northern line, Poultry to Bank. The annotated landing, one step the first, next step the first.

Here where my arm reaches your arm, a sparrow calls to me. Hark it cried and rises to the gutter from its bath – dust and the glitter of a common day – glory and trash – the common rag-bird – a slut in tweeds – an acrobat.

What is consonance between a sparrow and a fool? What is the song of cartwheels? Here is telegraphed the vowels of a missing demi-urge – the varnish that reveals the heart grain of the mildewed veneer.

A dog might shit before the Queen – moving from Pall Mall to avoid the crowds, into Buckingham House – the King between Buck and Ham – *noli me tangere* shouts the Earl of Sandwich – that is mine to eat – the rest of you can fuck off to St. James's.

When the underground surfaced by the two pools – engineered to transport the steaming futurity – fish were boiled alive and ducks poached in their muddy puddles. Wellsprings – once the haunt of Chatterton and Claude became the depository closet for the infantry – towels and breeches cast off in a huff.

Saddled on either side of his horse, Coleridge brought the tea tray into the fountain without much meaning to – stood eventually akimbo the staling horse would never shift again. Honestly it never occurred to him to dismount until Sebastian shrugged and the whole show came tumbling down.

The fool then, with his gift of eloquence – star mapping the plaza as Maud and Francine canoodle over zabaglione. With deft flicks of his juti he lifts the sleeping stray off the balustrade and into the fountain basin – for as he well knows, such minor atrocities test the theory of causal relations. His own view is that his own view is nothing of the sort.

In doing so he changes everything and nothing, for nothing happened that was not possible, and in happening it had of course happened. Had the cat remained sleeping on the lichened stone, ah well then, we shall never know – although if we hold ourselves a feather's breadth away from ourselves we might just hear the passing possibility of all possibilities including the dozing feline resting for eternity on her stolid platform.

Eventually one must jump back to where one never left. Even the idea of leaving was here. But of course here is nowhere at all. So the fool might as well place himself in the most beautiful of nowheres, because beauty is the herald of proximity, and proximity is all we nearly have on this spinning orb. A fountain then, with its series of concentric circles and then with its water flowing in and out of a spot, a spout a spigot on the centre spot of the city – and all the while the world spinning and all the while the drawing by Piranesi of Piranesi drawing the fountain with the fool dancing past his frozen cat – her closed eye an omphalus – her whistling snore an anthem to the infinite.

The drops of water scattered over the surface cause a reflection on the floor of the fountain's pool of a pattern loosely resembling a quincunx, coming into and drifting out of existence. Light bends through the ripples to create shadows of the wave formation on the surface – the quincunx might also be the pattern on the side of the scaly-looking pineapples rendered in stone at each corner of the fountain's balustrade, those as well falling slowly out of shape.

A ghost might drift around the fountain lip – the cat agitates, for a cat has not excluded fanciful ideas from its habitude. The sun we call it, but the light really, from an evening angle, touches the water drops and illuminates the whole like a liquid chandelier. This is not an accidental happenstance – the plaza is to be considered the reception room of the city. Here the fool is the master of ceremonies, greeting his guests, to wit, not a soul.

Wearing her swimmers cap entitled 'The Azeleas of Nacogdoches' she opens her hymnal to the waves: Lyrics of the Langoustines. Which might have been misheard. Leery of the Langour Steens

She had to hum along as the Chorus had already begun – but her own hum, following minutely behind filled her ears with a pattern of dissonance, like a defeating echo on a party-line phone call – and the chorus faded like a whistling troop marching out of the barracks.

Where are they going, these young men dressed in pomp. All that they know is that they must march in sequence, part of a machine whose purpose is to function. What it does and who it does it for are questions beyond the nut and the bolt. Even the on-button has no knowledge of the blind fingertip pointing towards its smooth indented greenness. We might call it god, in the guise of King & Country. But then again someone might have leant against it. A sleeping cat stirred by a ghost. We whistle the tune because we do not know the words.

Leery of the langoustines she sings – leery of their underbellies, leery of their faces – whiskered for the shallows.

A jack of hearts – what can it mean, as surely it must if any sign is to have meaning, all signs must. We might play privileges and preferences, but all signs are there to be read. A jack-of –hearts on the floor of the underground carriage. Abandoned or left – both. The fool has read of someone compiling a full deck from such happy finds. Perhaps they are a few cards short of a full deck, so to speak. What are the chances of that? Preposterous. No chance. Sooner find life on a planet like this – microbes converting to sentient beings with enough time during the hard task of survival to invent games and toys and playing cards. His friends must have colluded – loaded the underground with various missing cards – waiting for the coup de grace on his 50th birthday. The Jack–of-hearts dropped for him by his feverishly excited wife – long-suffering, ready for the next chapter. There isn't one. The fool pockets the card. What can it mean?

The image of an engineer entering and re-entering the crypt – or the image of an engraver etching and re-etching the crypt. The crypt is like the grave – emptied with epitaph – the etching, the Mausoleum and the crypt – an image of the engraver engraving his own grave.

Rum it is, a rum affair. Oscar with his whistle pig greased and bloodied. Fill the tub with boiling water, add bicarbonate of soda and some kitchen foil – pour the family silver in and watch: immediately you will see fizzing – the sulfur transfers allegiancy from the aluminium – the tarnish, silver sulfide, lifts, the clouds disperse and a faery moon emerges into night.

The German word "meineid," false oath, a pseudo-poem – Orpheus singing with loss of faith, his lover is lost, the maenads tear him limb from limb, but he's still whistling. How infuriating! They chuck his head in the Hebrus.

In the narrowing street the fool laments his death – floating as he is, headless along the alley wall. The night sky is an unnamable mix of plum yellow – the shadows by the halo of the wedding cake yellow
80

lamppost is nacreous mauve – nowhere is the palette more extreme than the gorgeous ochre bricks – settled for the night into drab after a day of ruddy triumph.

The fool fucks too nicely. What the fuck. It's meant to be a fucking release not a thank you card! Hard cock-shout whose fucking idea was it to be well behaved. Not yours surely!

The trowel in the lent upright position gets pointlessly kicked over even though someone planned to put it there so what? It's not tragic – the trowel placed by the two empty flower pots can fall over – a mother can drop the disguise – can hate her child – a child can notice the world not giving a fuck and it still goes on.

The night owl that sees all this does not live in that city. Not like many birds has he become extinct. He lives in nothing like a city but a spectrum of evolving contours. The eye orbed like a musical Magellan – a mask paraded before the jury are themselves decapitated on the rough granite tiles. When blood flows for the owl it is nothing personal because nothing personal has ever existed – the rat that pulls the wiring from the starter motor – the blasted impact on its high neck shoulder as the shadow thuds right through to the next image on the spectrum.

A night bus – those aboard seeming even to themselves to be part of the night bus spectacle as if this were how Nations are born. We can only hold onto moments of self before they become laughably unlike experience. A child might take the same thing out of the special box in an identical sequence – it's the night bus, the N7 and I am perhaps given this role once more – an event so like a repetition I might not need to be frightened of dying.

Bus rounding Fountain square. Huddled dark hulk of sleeping homeless which we decide is not us so we turn away to the next involvement. A black cat running across the zebra crossing, here not here, here not here, here not here. What are those bollards by Thorntons doing? Some flowers on the curb. A single playing card lent there with purpose?

Every true artist is annihilated in the making of art – this is a truism that leaves every piece of art the cross of the resurrection. Some pieces actually depict the resurrection. So perhaps all of them do.

27,000 shames on myself at the wedding of a friend. I have no right to be. Each moment is a mask – identical to the self. He might whistle himself to sleep. It sounds familiar, the soldiers leaving the barracks when he was a boy. The Barracks long gone. The soldiers longer gone. The tune still here. What are those words?

> Darling darling
> pass me by the railings,
> give me your hand for the ball,
> if I can't have you
> nobody should have you
> dancing with one and all

Okay, if consciousness is not internal, then where is memory? Well? Where? Here?

The owl awakens to the drone (an engine), then a bang (the moped it is on), it has no idea having flown into a barbed wire fence the night before.

And after that chocolate popcorn. She should not, but at 75 who now cares about a little bit more to love, not that love has ever been forthcoming, Maud perhaps, but neither mother nor the father (absent to be honest). Brother dead in the war of course.

The fool stands with the few bystanders, leery of the langoustine. 50 years of age and sleeping by a fountain.

If I am dying, why am I hearing that song? I can almost remember the words, a slight bubble at her lips, a lisping whistle. The whistle pig, the whistle pig, who has seen the whistle pig? Here on its blister pad, leery of the langoustine, leering at the lounging Queen, Queer in her eiderdown, Darling take my hand.

III.

Withers

Contaminated light (idea of purity therefore) burst open today. In dying we produce narration. My hope etc. The B + W photo documentary of colleges and Bridges, Naves and enclosures. Temperature controls creativity and time. Light slows down. How. Expansion must take into account (and form) collapses. Other lovers in their exchange, but not my involvement. That pleasure hers (can) not mine. Death again. Sleeping in the nighttime blue light she heard me enter the room and pulls the sheet to cover herself – which is even more engaging than not knowing, or doing. Example of misleading linguistic excitement. Soldiers arm in arm – their tongues – transcontinental arsenal – mosque penetrations – alarums – firing pins cocked? Do they? Interesting cunt (try interesting for size) kicked in. Such assertions of violence merely recorded – pruriently – for armchair viewing. How does that make you feel. Any of it. I can't say. Cobwebs exist in all states. Or countries. In the atmosphere they can descend on. Washed cars. What are we together. What are our trophies. The indigenous household gods in the U.S. are T.V. movie actors. Act as omens. But in this case the lives aren't the outcome. My responsibilities are governmental. My own account. Anybody's business. A sense of balance. Soaring. Ecstatic. Debt. Dislodged in the motor lodge with color t.v. by Univision. Something like that. On the flight over. The over is an instant of receptive articulation – like here, or being. What we are over is not in question. We have been brought. What we are over is never in question if everything remains in balance – politics, human nature, physics, machine construction. How was the flight over.

Shoulder to shoulder. They. The soldiers together. Can this postured gendering result in anything but an eruption of the erotic. Swathed with sucking a limp. The pocket's contents. Bedford Park, 4 bd, 2 bth. Wellesley Rd 2 bd 1bth. Arlington Gdns. The American imagination is vast and empty. Its only mode of expression is oppositional. Popular white Christianity Puritanism filtered through several layers of materialism and opposed communism (self-interest). The cowboy is a wandering fool. Redundant machismo. The American outlaw steals for himself. The film actor seems larger than life but is smaller. The only heroes are the risen underprivileged. But they have brought nothing with them. Slavery ended with racism and black poverty. The defining features of the woman's life: marriage and weight-gain.

From the outside domesticity looks enticing. The terrace houses decorated for the holidays. The littered shelves in the study. Two milk bottles on the step. Dark mat of leaves – boot cleaner – takeaway flyer – taxi business card – are you interested. Do you need. A fire can die out. I am I suppose made of milk like a large thrush's breast packed with life. Speckled. And spear points in a garden. In scarlet town where I was born & the cruel dead dog upon the mat. This battle fares like the morning's war. The great 18th c. Eng. Paintings. The English-bible. Milton business. The hill and the grass inseperable the lowly English artist digging his work out like a turnip. Then all that aristocratic flummery. The European baubles. Off into clouds then. No blood. No fucking. Migraines and face powder. Poodles licking a pox. A fish leaping I witness a flood. A bit of a thunder cloud behind the apple tree. Ploughing the fields you can see from my window a rare white venus (found among sundry writing tools locked in their box). I gave away things that mattered to me to people that mattered to me at the time which I now regret. Though in truth I regret the loss. Reclaimable. What else. Moans and sobs which I can hardly make out. Next door. Is this how I'm heard. A desire to locate. Themselves. In others. The difference. Between. Withers.

Spells. I am conjuring. One goes that way. One this. I'm bashing my head against. Myself. Let's change we say. And then we open up the envelope. In 19th century letter writing. where the author. Is the servant. Yours. Etc. The freedom to wander. The city at night. Under cover of darkness. Of cultured exploration (exploitation). The present era mocking the repression of the previous eras. Round of applause. Apple sauce. As if there were a knot in my mind that I might untie. I had access to one. Try to imagine it as something else. A tree bending in the air. But it's a bottle neck of desires. Trumped up no doubt. A knotty tree bough on borrowed land. The wire fence that whistles the length of the path with snags of wool. Enough. To make. a difference. In all probability. waves. collapse. On the beach. Below. You see. From your window. The fern. Withers.

A nest. It had been delicately made. For a temporary stay. Which is all we have. Any sense of. Not as a home so much as a crib. A cot I'd say. Being English. But not anymore. Living somewhere else. Without access. To local identity. My sense of place unloosed. My sense of self. Withers.

The angels that hang washing. or the saints at hoeing. Observed correctly. Is agony. Is the distance between objects ever. Complete. You notice. Touching yourself. Regularly. Without care. It's a map of where we are. Maps change. They become redundant. Material such as parchment is too unstable. The ancient becomes precious. Suggesting the possibility of survival. Each new leaf perfect. It. Withers.

When we display ourselves. Which we loathe. For consumption. By our friends. At a later time. And know they will make of us. beyond our control. There are sparks. And crinkles in the spine. Silver flash. down by the river. Watching the light. On the surface. Sparkle. Mesmerized. Too brief. To take hold. No better. view. of the water. And loosestrife. Weeping willow. In its own shadow. Clover and dandelion. Withers.

[Poetic interlude]

Recusatio: A refusal to write epics

Let us say that Love is its own war
Or that a small farm will suffice
We will not fight at Actium
In service to our owner's whim
Today the farm is toxic to the land
Just as the early frost and drought
My heart will be a fruit that cannot grow
Plucked early for some hidden store
(too late for the festival, or too early for)

IV.

Monadic Vistas

The cassowary inconsolable,
the plangent duck ablaze
up stately troops of Myanmar!
sporting a Rangoon grace

Tea less sweet tho' strong
a nursery screen a rope
tea in a china bowl
a lizard in the mint

Choked utterly by history
prostrate by distempered walls
the wind and sun approximately
over the ha-ha'd lawn

Everyone prefers their own monkey
Eventually you disappear
Naked in the old man's studio
Sitting awkward on a wooden chair

The queerest fish walking the land
The fishermen searching the sea
Fair to me are distant songs of joy
I thought I knew so much of love

Old men should be left to the tigers
one last fury, one last futile moan
and at the side of a heavenly fish
I throw my heart into the sky

The beast-whore behemoth & leviathan
hills to the ocean floor
above the mountain teeth
the sky teeth meet.

Wade freely – quailing at the dice
faithfully thrown
your mother dies
your father imitates bland charities (convenient to our disguise)

Azure on a bended "O"
The sadness settled in the lid
And like the sun turning the globe
The self poured out its bland selfhood

...and then the cavalry descended into view
I do not know the scope of what I see
A landscape scene engraved in miniature
An evening cloud seen through an open door

Drop now down to the golden shrine
The kitchen fire where family ghosts shelter
Drop like the liquid shades
Onto the altering surface of the day

Mother swaps anxiety with daughter
Father worn dumb by his many failures
Son waits at departure's door
(all heaven is made of such characters)

Artemis – mother of all hares
Calchas sees the womb ripped out
 – she cannot now forgive her fate
Apollo's eagles ravenously bent

Whether I of this high wall
or of pure will ascend
and so my self – thus circumscribed
might live my mind exactly there defined

The wheel of Ixion stood still
& Tantalus ignored the waves
Tityus sat unmolested in his cloak
Sisyphus took leisure on his stone

*

And without sun? And what of that?
And god we know without
A drop of water – or say snow
When snow is needed – and it is

And without rain, or care or
Fainting goats – a transport
Without shoes or cows or cobwebs
Without shit or corn or eyes

We know we fail – and without
Empty I the brine of apathy
God help the turkey and the duck
God help the mermaid and
The waiter and the sun

*

206-boned cabinet
with leather purse
& pearl-ringed jewel
and note descriptive of a soul

The small grace that keeps me afloat
When in expansive avenues of joy
The arms of sycamores seem
Held up in eternal ecstasy

But ravaged by a word or look
The arms are brittle sticks
That cannot reach nor save
The grace that slips away

I'm crushed today by emptiness
talking to the few people I love
or think I do. I'm tired to be
so little after all, and endlessly

a beautiful and bearded woman
in a cape of rose and gold
her throne of ivory split open
her fissure filled with corn

It is a rare stew
I'm placed upon
A bubble bursting at the rim
A rabbit baking in the sun

A sylph skips down the tessellated hall
A rock might crush a butterfly
But be assured they are not fragile but robust
Buffeted thus in an international storm

Mascaras out of the formal
The wind that is carried
Might animate a human soul
Birds, unnatural to the area
Green & excitable, their foreign accents execrable

The plums are dim at dusk
Like blind babies at the teat
The plums at night are blue
Under the shade of Montserrat

Like a lead bulb in the pond
The light of an empty cup
Cold in the summer night
And quiet off the beaten path

The swallow meets its shadow/at the pool
The ochre wall cut by the /curving blue
The cedars stand in groups/around midday
To offer solace to/the dragonflies

Eulàlia of the 13 geese
Rolled in a barrel of broken glass
Mexican Hambuerguesas
Emperors y Labourers

Terrible Catholic night
Steepled in Glory aghast
Hot altars & erogeny ere
The erect merchant kneels

*

my tower hungry
I'm so very
Lenient – to one side
Inside out

Silents silentium blue public
that whistles tiny whistles
of the passing wistful here
is a shopfront filled with whims
Here is an empty photograph
To furrow homelessly

…vegetable glass
ground out of green
well water poured
from crucible lips

wipe with despair
the verdigris lens
Station des Weges
La lunette de Paris…

In the midnight blue steel void
yourself away collapsible
the craft between the glass
and sunken sea-green air –

London to London via tube
illusion of light empty space
grey coats yellow evening light
pavemental movementum aspic glow

*

A legless Moon
Wading in the pool
When I was young
I knew

Driven past Halifax at night
The ember lights of farm buildings
A lorry shadows by. When we arrive
The cold air opening another day

the orange peel blooms
on the carpet
reach out a hand
dear Mother gone

Herophilia
The Sybil at Cumae
who lived a thousand years
and wished to die

dust has closed her eyes
and dirt her ears
her smile is lost to us
covered by soil

kneel at the beach
or at the grave
a bird will find you out
the ocean wave

in last year's nest
the toaster reaching in
no birds return
the bread will burn

plucked from a river
wishing to be god
or the least of things
a sop of bread on top

what I was
was the experience of
(represented as memorial to)
this one organic self

the frequent stags
and beetles in
the grass domed
emptiness called home

perfectly happy   perfectally still
where I am
landlord of a lizard
master of a fly

soft though as mellow
death is
still the silent monster
we all follow

It is impossible – things non-existent
that won't go away
a single bat I saw 3 yrs ago
flickering across the estuary

CPSIA information can be obtained
at www.ICGtesting.com
Printed in the USA
FSHW010210090319
56083FS

9 781848 616448